Pollution

by Helen Orme

By Helen Orme

Series consultant: Terry Jennings

ticktock editor: Sophie Furse

ticktock designer: Hayley Terry

Picture research: Lizzie Knowles

With thanks to: Mark Sachner, Joe Harris and Claire Lucas

Copyright © ticktock Entertainment Ltd 2008
First published in Great Britain in 2008 by ticktock Media Ltd,
Unit 2, Orchard Business Centre, North Farm Road,
Tunbridge Wells, Kent, TN2 3XF

ISBN 978 1 84696 735 1 pbk
Printed in China

Picture credits
AP/ PA Photos: 14. John Cancalosi/ Nature Picture Library/ Rex Features: 28b. Corbis/ Photolibrary Group: 30. Creatas/
SuperStock: 19c. Alexander Hafemann/ iStock: 24c. Andrew Howe/ iStock: 17t. Sander Kamp/iStock: 6-7. Efrem Lukatsky/
AP/ PA Photos: 21. Hans F. Meier/ iStock: 29t. Ben Osborne/ Getty Images: OFC. Richard Packwood/ Oxford Scientific: 8b.
Photodisc: OBC, 1, 2, 11t, 23t, 31. Shutterstock: 7t, 9, 12-13, 16-17, 22-23, 24b, 25c, 25b, 26, 27b, 28t, 32. R Sherwood
Veith/ iStock: 10-11. Dr Ian Snape: 29b. Stephen Strathdee/ iStock: 4-5. Leah Warkentin/ Design Pics Inc/ Rex Features: 18.
Chris Wilkins/ AFP/ Getty Images: 15. Michael S. Yamashita/ Corbis: 13t. Courtesy of www.victorianlondon.org: 27t.
Every effort has been made to trace the copyright holders, and we apologise in advance for any unintentional omissions.
We would be pleased to insert the appropriate acknowledgements in any subsequent edition of this publication.

CONTENTS

Words that appear **in bold** are explained in the glossary.

WHAT IS POLLUTION?

Pollution *can hurt every living thing on our planet! It happens whenever something harmful or poisonous is put into the* **environment**.

Pollution can affect the air we breathe, when smoke and other chemicals are released into the **atmosphere**. When chemicals are dumped into our rivers and oceans, the pollution from them can affect the water we drink and the food we eat. It can also kill birds and other animals and prevent plants from growing.

Pollution can also get into the soil, especially when too many **pesticides** and chemical **fertilisers** are used on farmland. There, it may also affect both the food we eat and the health of plants and animals.

AIR POLLUTION – SMOG

One very common type of pollution is smog. Smog can hang over cities like a dark cloud. It makes it very difficult to see objects in the distance.

Smog is a mixture of smoke and fog. It happens when a layer of warm, heavy air stops polluted air from rising. This is why it's often smoggy on hot summer days, when pollution from traffic and chimneys builds up around cities. When this happens, harmful chemicals are trapped near the ground, and we breathe them in.

Smog can make your eyes, nose, and throat sore, and can make it hard to breathe. Over many years, air pollution can harm people's lungs and may even cause lung cancer.

LONDON SMOG

Smog used to be a serious problem in London. In 1952, as many as 12,000 Londoners may have died from the effects of smog. The problem was solved when officials banned the burning of coal within the city.

Bangkok is a city in Thailand which suffers badly from smog.

GREENHOUSE GASES

We have seen how pollution can become trapped in Earth's atmosphere. Some gases also trap warm air. These are called **greenhouse gases**.

Burning **fossil fuels**, such as coal, oil or gas, adds greenhouse gases to our atmosphere. Without greenhouse gases, it would be too cold for us to survive. However, the buildup of greenhouse gases is now causing Earth to warm up too much. This is called **global warming**.

Global warming may cause **drought** in some places. It could also cause ice at the North and South Poles to melt. This would make the sea rise and cause flooding.

ACID RAIN

Burning fossil fuels releases a chemical that can pollute moisture in the air. The result is **acid rain**, a very dangerous substance that can damage plants and buildings hundreds of kilometres from its source.

RIVER POLLUTION

For thousands of years, many people have used rivers for drinking, doing laundry, and cooking. River water polluted by chemicals and sewage can make people sick, and those people may in turn pass on their illnesses to others.

In order to grow more crops, farmers sometimes use fertilisers and pesticides on their fields. When it rains, these chemicals may be washed into nearby rivers.

Pesticides kill wildlife in the river. Fertilisers can make fast-growing weeds and **algae** grow even faster. The weeds and algae use up oxygen as they grow. They use up even more oxygen when they die and rot. This means that there is not enough oxygen for the animals in the river to breathe.

Algae turns rivers green.

Harmful waste water from factories is sometimes poured straight into rivers.

POLLUTED OCEANS

People once thought that anything dumped into the ocean would harmlessly disappear. Today we know better!

Many of the same chemicals that pollute rivers also end up in the ocean. Fertilisers washed into rivers may go out into the ocean and cause fast-growing algae. These **organisms** use up oxygen needed by other living things. As in rivers, too much algae can lead to the death of plants that sea creatures depend on for their survival.

Today, untreated sewage and chemicals from factories cause most of the pollution in our oceans. These pollutants poison sea life and can make swimmers and surfers sick.

MERCURY POISONING IN JAPAN

These people are protesting against a factory in Japan which released **mercury** into the sea from 1932 to 1968. This poison built up in people who ate fish **contaminated** by the mercury. Over 2,000 people became seriously ill from mercury poisoning.

The Valero oil refinery on the island of Aruba. In 2006, a broken pipe in the refinery caused an oil spill.

OIL SPILLS AT SEA

Crude oil is black, sticky, and deadly to wildlife. Large amounts of it can ruin beaches and destroy ocean life.

Oil pollution is often caused by oil tankers. Some of these ships release oil when they wash out their tanks into the ocean. Releasing oil into the ocean on purpose is illegal.

One of the worst oil disasters happened in 1989, when the tanker *Exxon Valdez* hit a reef in Alaska, USA. The oil slick that came from the ship may have killed more than 250,000 seabirds and other animals.

Workers cleaning up one of the polluted beaches after the Exxon Valdez disaster.

POLLUTING THE LAND

Chemicals used to grow crops
don't just pollute rivers and seas.
They also affect life on land and in
the air.

As well as killing weeds, weed killers
also destroy plants that do not harm
crops. Many insects eat these plants,
and they may be killed by the pesticides.

Chemicals can stay in the bodies of birds
and animals that eat contaminated crops
or insects for a long time.

Some chemicals sprayed on land can
also be spread by the wind. Scientists
worry that these chemicals may make
us sick if they end up on our food.
We could also get sick from eating meat
from animals fed contaminated crops.

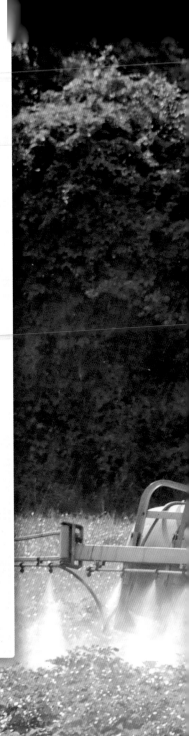

BIRDS AT RISK

When pesticides were first used, many birds, such as this sparrow hawk, were killed by poisons that were found in the bodies of the animals they ate. Today these types of pesticide are illegal.

A crane at work on a landfill.

LANDFILL SITES

Land pollution also takes the form of rubbish and litter. People make lots of rubbish, so where does it all go?

Many cities dump rubbish in big holes in the ground. When these holes, called **landfills**, are full, the landfill is covered with soil. Then grass is planted.

This sounds like a good idea, but the waste may contain chemicals that contaminate the ground. Today, some cities are using plastic sheets to stop chemicals leaking into the soil.

Eventually the rubbish is covered over with soil and grass.

Even rotting food can add to pollution. As food rots, it produces methane. Methane is a greenhouse gas. Too much methane in the atmosphere can add to global warming.

RADIOACTIVE POLLUTION

*Nuclear power is a 'clean' energy source.
No fossil fuels are burned to create this kind of
energy, so no greenhouse gases are made.
However, the waste from nuclear power stations
can harm living things.*

All nuclear power stations produce nuclear waste.
This waste can contaminate the soil for thousands of
years. To prevent this, it must be stored and disposed
of carefully.

CHERNOBYL

In April 1986, there was an
explosion at the Chernobyl
nuclear power station in
Ukraine, a country in Eastern
Europe. Radioactive dust and
gas spread through the
atmosphere and into
rainwater. Plants, animals, and
people were poisoned by the
radiation. Many people
became very ill and died.

*The red arrow shows the direction in
which winds carried the radioactive
cloud just after the accident.*

This monument in Kiev remembers the many people who lost their lives in the Chernobyl disaster.

LIGHT POLLUTION

The bright lights of our cities and towns may not seem like a form of pollution. However, light pollution affects both people and animals.

Light pollution can stop some people from sleeping. It is also a problem for astronomers trying to look at the night sky. The bright lights make it hard to see the stars!

Animals may be confused into thinking it is daytime instead of nighttime. Some migrating birds use the stars to find their way. Light pollution can make them become lost, and even injure themselves flying into buildings.

NOISE POLLUTION

Noise from traffic, planes, or machinery can be just as serious as other forms of pollution. It can cause health problems by interfering with our concentration and sleep.

RENEWABLE AND CLEANER ENERGY

There are ways to make energy without producing greenhouse gases or smoke. However, at the moment there's no perfect way.

• **Wind turbines** are a very clean way of producing energy. The drawback is that they only work when the wind blows.

• Solar energy uses light from the Sun to make energy. Unfortunately, it doesn't work at night!

• Tidal power uses the flow of the tides to make energy. It is clean and reliable. However, cities that need the energy may be a long way from the ocean.

• Nuclear power stations do not produce greenhouses gases, but they do produce radioactive waste, which can be very dangerous.

A wind turbine

• **Hydroelectric power** stations use the force of water rushing downhill or trapped behind dams. Only some places are hilly enough, though, and dams are very large and can harm the environment.

A hydroelectric dam

GET OUT OF YOUR CAR!

Traffic fumes can cause serious pollution. Some people think electric cars may be the best way to reduce the pollution produced by petrol. The electricity to charge the cars' batteries usually comes from power stations that burn fossil fuels. However, electric cars still cause less pollution than cars powered by petrol.

Here are some ideas to help you save on car journeys:

• Buy things from shops near your home, and buy food that is grown locally.

• Use public transport whenever you can.

• Walk or cycle – it's good for the environment and your health.

Help the environment by walking!

What people who have to drive cars can do:

• Slow down! Driving fast uses more petrol.

• Drive a smaller, more efficient car.

• Share a car with other people who go to school or work with you.

What carmakers can do to make cars less polluting:

• Make hybrid cars, which have petrol engines and electric motors.

• Design cars with engines that switch off when the car is not moving.

• Find new, clean fuels that don't cause pollution.

ORGANIC FARMING: FERTILISER-FREE GOODNESS

Most shops and supermarkets sell organic fruit, vegetables, and meat. What does 'organic' mean?

• Organic fruits, vegetables, and meat are produced in a more natural way. The soil is not treated with chemical pesticides or fertilisers. Animals are not given chemicals to make them grow bigger.

• Growing organic fruit and vegetables and breeding animals without using chemicals helps keep the environment cleaner and safer. Many people believe organic food is tastier, too.

• Organic fruits and vegetables cost more than non-organic produce. So why not grow your own at home?

• Even in a small garden there is room for a few vegetables. And even without a garden, herbs and small salad vegetables such as tomatoes and cucumbers can be grown in a window box, or even in a flowerpot on a windowsill.

Growing things to eat is fun – and they taste delicious!

CLEAN RIVERS:
CASE STUDY – THE RIVER THAMES FIRE

The River Thames flows through London. In the 1700s, it was clean and full of fish.

As the city grew, the river got dirtier. Then things suddenly got even worse. In the 1840s, flushing toilets became popular. So houses were connected to drains. This meant that after a person flushed, the sewage went through drains that emptied right into the Thames! By 1850, the river was so smelly you had to hold your nose when you walked over a bridge!

An 1850 illustration showing foul-smelling 'Father Thames'.

The problem was finally solved in the 1860s. Huge sewers were built to take the waste right out of the city. Now the Thames is as clean as it was 250 years ago.

The River Thames in 2008 – sewage free!

LITTER DAMAGE

Litter is horrible to look at. It can also be deadly to wildlife. There are many ways that rubbish can harm other living things. Here are a few:

• Small animals can sometimes climb into glass or plastic bottles. If the inside of the bottle is too slippery for them to get out, they can starve to death.

This litter is a danger to wildlife.

• Animals can get their heads stuck in plastic cartons or in the plastic rings that are used to carry packs of bottles or cans. If the carton or ring is tight enough, it can choke an animal.

• Broken glass can cut animals as it passes through their digestive system.

• A piece of glass lying in a field or a forest can act like a magnifying glass when sunlight passes through it, and start a fire.

• Remember, glass and plastic don't rot. If you dump them, they may be there forever!

Animals can get trapped in plastic bags.

LAWS ABOUT POLLUTION

One of the best ways to stop pollution is to get the government to make new laws. There are already laws against polluting the air, land, and water, but some people think they are not strict enough. If you feel strongly about an issue, you could write a letter to your local MP, and ask your friends to sign it.

Think big – you can make a difference!

Some laws affect places that don't belong to one country – like the oceans, and Antarctica. Every country has to agree to these laws.

Antarctica is the cleanest place on Earth. Without strict laws, however, the land and the seas around it would soon become seriously polluted.

Wilkes Station, Antarctica was a research station that opened in 1957. It became contaminated by leaking fuel containers and was closed down in 1969. It has been buried under ice for years. However, sometimes during a thaw, you can see some of the old buildings and the rubbish that was left behind! People are now working hard to clean up Antarctic pollution.

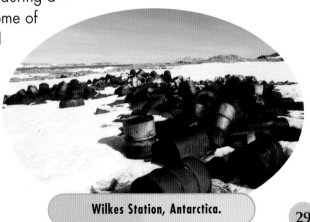

Wilkes Station, Antarctica.

29

HOW YOU CAN HELP

• With the help of a teacher or another responsible adult, collect litter from your school and make a display of it. (Be sure to show your teacher what you want to collect before you pick it up. Be especially careful not to handle broken glass or any other dangerous objects.) How much of the litter could have been recycled?

• Contact your local council or MP to find out how pollution is tackled in your area.

Collecting rubbish makes the environment more pleasant for everyone.

• Try to get your parents to buy food that is produced locally and does not have too much packaging.

• Always recycle! Make sure that any waste you produce is put in its proper container.

Visit these websites for more information about pollution, litter and recycling.

The Young People's Trust for the Environment:
www.ypte.org.uk

EcoFriendlyKids: www.ecofriendlykids.co.uk

GLOSSARY

acid rain Rain, snow, or other moisture that contains a high amount of acid because of pollution.

algae Simple green plants, including seaweed, that mostly grow in water.

atmosphere The thick layer of air that surrounds the Earth.

contaminated Made impure or harmful by pollution.

drought A long period when there is much less rainfall than usual, or even no rain at all.

environment The conditions that affect a living thing – including climate, soil, and other life forms.

fertilisers Materials that are used to help plants grow.

fossil fuels Fuels such as gas, oil, and coal, made from living things that died millions of years ago.

global warming The warming of the planet's air and oceans as a result of a build-up of greenhouse gases in the atmosphere.

greenhouse gases Gases such as carbon dioxide that warm the planet by stopping heat escaping from the atmosphere into space.

hydroelectric power Electricity produced using the force of falling water.

landfills Big holes in the ground that are filled with rubbish and waste.

mercury A poisonous silver-coloured metal that is usually liquid.

organisms Living plants, animals, or other life forms.

pesticides Chemicals that kill insects and other pests that damage crops.

pollution Harmful substances that are released into the environment.

radioactive When something sends out radiation. Radiation causes dangerous changes in living things.

wind turbines Machines that turn the power of the wind into electricity. These look a little like windmills.

INDEX